A Va

CW00509624

Poetry from the Pantry of Life

Published by Red Lizard Books

Printed in the UK

Copyright © Carol Ellis 2020

About the author

Carol Ellis, who writes under the pen
name Mrs Yorkshire the Baking Bard,
was born in 1962 in Wakefield, West
Yorkshire to Irish parents.

She has been married to Michael since
1985 and they have one daughter, Jessica,
born in 1991 and a grandson, Charles,
born in 2020. She has been living on the
Isle of Man since 2007.

She is a performing poet, infamous for
her stand-up style of comedy in rhyme.

Her poetry has featured in many local
and national newspapers, in magazines
and on *Channel 5's* daytime shows *The
Wright Stuff* and *The Jeremy Vine Show.*
She also has a regular slot on *Manx
Radio's Late Lunch* reading her poetry.

She is regularly invited into both primary
and secondary schools to give poetry
workshops and performs at many charity
and corporate events.

She writes observational poetry and
her cleverly-crafted poems are both
humorous, witty and will have you
roaring with laughter. She brings
ordinary subjects to life through the
rhythmical creation of beauty in words.

(Cont...)

Her social media presence has gathered much interest, especially since the introduction of her daily *Words of Wit & Wisdom.* Having started writing a rhyming couplet a day over a year ago she is currently working on a book of her *Words of Wit and Wisdom* and a special edition of *Festive Words of Wit and Wisdom* which will both be available in the autumn of 2020. Her popular trilogy of books *A Slice of Humour, Food for Thought* and *Sugar and Spice* are still proving popular and are available to buy from Amazon and bookshops.

Acknowledgements

Thank you to my husband, Michael, for all the hard work formatting my books in preparation for publication and for your support every day.

To Graeme Hogg for your wonderful illustrations. You never cease to amaze me. I present to you with many challenges and you always manage to surpass my expectations.

To all my friends in the Isle of Man Poetry Society who have supported, advised and encouraged me, for the fun we've had along the way and the friendships we've made.

To Chris Payne of Effort-Free Media. You encouraged me to connect with my followers on social media on a daily basis which gave me the idea to write and post a two-line rhyming couplet every day. This has proved to be a huge success. Thank you for inspiring me to publish books in the first place and for your invaluable advice, guidance and, of course, your friendship.

(Cont...)

Thank you to all my friends and family and of course to my many followers who check in daily to read my words of wit and wisdom as well as my full-length poems on all the social media platforms. Thank you for the feedback and kind comments I receive. It really does make it all worthwhile and encourages me to write more.

A special thank you to my daughter, Jessica and her husband David, for presenting Michael and I with our first grandchild, Charles Michael, born in July this year. I'm sure he'll inspire me to write some 'Nannie-themed' poetry and his arrival has been a wonderful highlight in what has been a very strange year for everyone.

Illustrated by Graeme Hogg

www.thewholehogg.carbonmade.com

Cartoons, illustration & theming concept design.

Contents

A Little Light Refreshment
(A collection of humorous poems)

An Early Night 17
A Trip to the Orthopaedic Clinic ... 21
Haute Cuisine 25
A Christmas Message 29
New Year's Resolutions 33
A Very British Affair 37
A Lousy Dilemma 41
Your Mum's an Expert Spy 45

Something to Chew On
(A collection of thought-provoking poems)

Stand Up to Bullying 51
Invisible, Unseen, Unknown 55
Let's Kick Cancer's Arse 59
I'm Still Here 63
Dunblane 67
Another Day, Another Grave 71
Bloody Sunday 75
The Great Hunger 79
Beyond the Wall 83

Places to Relish
(A collection of poems about inspiring places)

An Irish Ballad 89
Magnificent Mayo 93
Magical Maughold 97
Royal Ramsey 101
My Wakefield Childhood 105

Something Sweet
(A collection of heartwarming poems)

The Magic of Books 111
What Christmas Means to Me 115
Let's Hear it for the Boys 119
From the Cradle to the Grave 123
Truth 127
The Parish Walk 131

A Bittersweet Affair
(A collection of poems inspired by the Covid-19 Pandemic of 2020)

Stay at Home 137
The Year the World Was Paused 141
Quarantine Quandaries 145
Isolation Revelation 149
Blue Poppies 153

A Letter from the Author
A Letter from the Author 157

A Little Light Refreshment

(A collection of humorous poems)

Early Night

Inspired by the late, great Victoria Wood's 'The Ballad of Barry and Freda'. I really enjoyed writing this poem and it's become a true crowd pleaser when performing it. If you're of a certain age, you'll probably relate to some, or even all of this poem. If you're a little younger, here's a glimpse into the future!

Early Night

Every night, just after tea
They settle down to watch TV
He reads the paper, watches Countdown
She goes up and turns the bed down

Once a genuine wild rover
Now he struggles to bend over
"An early night" was what she said
He looked at her with fear and dread

But her resolve was unremitting
She cleared the pots, put down her
knitting
He said "I can't 'cos I'm asthmatic
I need to watch *Cash in the Attic*

Don't forget I've got arthritis
Not to mention prostatitis
Blimey lass, you're off your rocker
I need to take my beta blocker"

Standing in her Damart vest
She knew that she was past her best
He looked upon her with despair
Observed her greying pubic hair

(Cont...)

They hadn't done it for a while
And tried to do it doggy style
Aggravating his bad knees
The whole performance made him
wheeze

Whichever way that she attacked it
Teased and coaxed it, even smacked it
They never really had a hope
Like playing snooker with a rope

She toyed with it, it didn't flinch
It didn't even move an inch
His spark had gone, without a doubt
He said "my pilot light's gone out"

The inclination soon diminished
He put her nightie down and finished
"The nights are dark, it's getting parky
We're much too old for this malarkey"

So every night just after tea
They settle down to watch TV
And after they're both washed and fed
They have a cup of tea instead!

A Trip to the Orthopaedic Clinic

In July 2018 I fell down Maughold Head, the headland next to the sea, which is a five minute walk from my house. I consequently ended up in plaster but was taken extremely good care of by the staff at Noble's Hospital in Douglas, Isle of Man. Thankfully, I made a full recovery. The following year I broke another bone and whilst I was waiting to see the orthopaedic consultant I was reading the posters on the wall. I was fascinated by the technical terminology and I woke up the next morning with rhymes spinning round in my head for all these wonderful words I'd read the previous day. I got up and immediately wrote this poem!

A Trip to the Orthopaedic Clinic

Stumbles, tumbles, slips and trips
Open fractures, broken hips
Drivers going far too fast
Ending up in plaster cast

Pains and sprains and tendonitis
Every kind of arthritis
Osteo and rheumatoid
A broken wrist, a cracked scaphoid

Tibs and fibs and metatarsals
Clavicles and painful carpals
Numerous humerus, vertebrae
They're all lined up in X-Ray

Every kind of diagnosis
Brittle bones and scoliosis
Folk with osteoporosis
Hoping for a good prognosis

A rather nasty dislocation
Needs reduction and fixation
Clinics packed with aches and breaks
Patients bringing cakes and bakes

(Cont...)

TT riders – very tough
Another torn rotator cuff
Athletes jumping over hurdles
Damaging their pelvic girdles

There's nothing that the docs can't do
To patch you up just like brand new
From accidents to wear and tear
You're guaranteed outstanding care

With TLC and bits of metal
Your bones will soon be in fine fettle
And just to put your mind at rest
The staff at Noble's are the best!

Haute Cuisine

*A couple of years ago, on my birthday,
my husband, Michael, took me out for a
meal to celebrate. Being a Yorkshireman,
he likes value for money. When his meal
arrived and the portions were, let's say,
meagre, he wasn't very pleased. To add
insult to injury, the waitress added a tip to
the bill! Needless to say, we never returned
to eat there again and Michael suggested
I write a poem about it. I've written this
from his point of view in a Yorkshire
dialect. So, altogether now, in your very
best Yorkshire accents…*

Haute Cuisine

I'm married to a Yorkshire girl, she's not a
bad old lass
She's always tea ont table and she's careful
wi' mi brass
She dunt spend owt on alcohol, she'd
rather 'ave a bun
And being vegetarian, she's proper cheap
to run

To celebrate her birthday, I took her for
a treat
And as it's only once a year, I thought I'd
do it reet
I dusted off mi wallet and I took her into
pub
And feeling proper generous, I bought
our lass some grub

She's always on a diet so she's never eaten
much
Although I like a well-stacked lass who's
softer to the touch
I told her "get thi snout in trough", dint
want her getting thinner
And I was feeling famished and was ready
for mi dinner

(Cont...)

But when the grub arrived well now the
portions were quite mean
The waitress duly told me this was known
as 'haute cuisine'
"Eee by gum tha must be daft" I said in
my defence
"Tha must think that I'm sackless and I've
got more brass than sense"

The chips were in a teacup you could
count 'em on one hand
And why the veg was rationed I just
couldn't understand
By 'eck it soon transpired that they were
then expecting tips
I gave 'em one – I told 'em to stop
skimping on the chips

So on our anniversary I 'ave a cunning
plan
I'll tek her on a day trip 'cos I'm such a
thoughtful man
Before we start ont journey, like a wise
and prudent chap
I'll set her on int kitchen and we'll tek us
bloomin' snap!

A Christmas Message

*If any of you use Facebook Messenger
or WhatsApp, you'll more than likely be
aware of so-called 'round robin' messages.
The sender sends a video or photo to all
their contacts at once. I don't know about
you but I find them extremely annoying,
especially at Christmas when, from the
beginning of December onwards, I receive
a deluge of flashing Christmas trees and
various festively adorned dancing teddy
bears. My annoyance is the inspiration for
the following poem.*

A Christmas Message

So now that it's December I am hearing
Christmas bells
The constant chime of messages are
casting wicked spells
That teddy with his mistletoe can stick it
up his arse
The scourge of viral greetings has become
a festive farce

Another childish video of superstitious
crap
Baby Jesus in his manger sings a
Christmas rap
Totally impersonal, the sender thinks
they're wacky
I don't believe in Jesus – if I did I'd find it
tacky

Another bloomin' 'slacktivist' who haunts
me for my 'crimes'
Apparently I'll die if I don't share it
twenty times
The planet is in peril and they've cursed
my life as well
But rest assured I'll take them with me all
the way to Hell

(Cont...)

So if I should ignore them do they think
I'm being rude?
Those dumb, annoying messages do not
enhance my mood
Before they press on 'send to all' at 2.00
a.m. when drunk
They should send something personal
and not recycled junk!

New Year's Resolutions

I don't know about you, but as soon we ring in the new year (usually with yet another deluge of 'Happy New Year' round robin messages), I start thinking about new year's resolutions. I'm sure many of you are the same. 2020 was a year that started off with good intentions but, of course, by March, everything went awry. Here's a poem about those new year's resolutions we all make and break. Let's hope 2021 is a little easier to navigate than 2020.

New Year's Resolutions

Another year has passed and it's
December 31st
I've eaten so much rubbish that I think
I'm fit to burst
Staying up till midnight for the young
ones is a treat
But when you're in your fifties it's
considered quite a feat

My new year's resolutions see me full of
good intention
I have so many vices, quite a few I
couldn't mention
Last year I gave up gambling, fed up of
taking chances
The odds were 3-1 it would be good for
my finances

I need to eat more healthily my clothes
are rather tight
But first I've cleared the cupboards, eating
everything in sight
I set a goal last year to lose a half a stone
or so
Ah well it could be worse I've only got a
stone to go

(Cont...)

Perhaps I should go jogging as a form of
exercise
But January's cold and wet I don't think
that it's wise
So once a week I'll bake a cake and ask
my friends to dinner
By March they'll all be fat and then I'm
bound to look much thinner

I know a bloke who thought he'd give the
dating game a go
He joined a cut-price agency, he found
them at Tesco
His new year's resolution was to get
himself wife
He should have been more careful 'cos
he got a 'bag for life'

So six weeks down the line I've broken
every resolution
I just don't have the willpower, I've come
to the conclusion
My Valentine bought chocolate, he is
such a thoughtful gent
I'll wait until next month – and then I'll
give it up for Lent!

A Very British Affair

Blimey, I've been so busy talking about the 'C' word this year that I've almost forgotten the 'B' word. In 2019 the UK voted to leave the EU and 'Brexit' inspired me to write this poem as an affectionate, tongue in cheek view of all things British.

A Very British Affair

An Englishman's home is his castle,
when all that is said and done
Those mad dogs and only Englishmen
go out in the midday sun
There'll always be an England, a green
and pleasant land
They've given two fingers to Europe and
finally taken a stand

Enough of these fanciful coffees, they're
having a nice cup of tea
No more of this darned coffee culture,
they'll be off to the pub now you see
They'll go to the farmers' markets, where
the best British produce is found
And they'll buy lots of nice bent
bananas, and they'll measure them out
by the pound

They've taken control of their borders,
that problem at last has been licked
They've finally found a solution, in the
six Irish counties they nicked
They'll go on the train to the seaside,
after forming an orderly queue
But they may venture outside of Engand,
just as long as their passport is blue

(Cont...)

They're partying hard on St George's
Day, just the same as the Home Nations
do
They're singing Bohemian Rhapsody,
you can bet they're all word perfect too
They've pulled out of Eurovision, it was
part of the Brexit divorce
They're so proud of The Stones and The
Beatles...and then P.J. and Duncan of
course

Anyone driving a German car has been
warned that they'll go to the Tower
Even the Royals are toeing the line 'cos
the tabloids possess all the power
Preparing to make Britain great again,
they've been told they're all in this
together
It's a shame they'll have nothing to
moan about but at least they can still
blame the weather!

A Lousy Dilemma

So, when the children returned to school in September, they were encouraged to observe good hygiene and endeavour to socially distance. This should reduce the risk of Covid infection. The good news is, it will probably reduce the risk of head lice too. Let's hope so anyway!

A Lousy Dilemma

So now the kids are back at school you'll
get some peace and quiet
You've joined a new hot yoga class and
started a new diet
You meet your mates for coffee and then
give the house a blitz
But when the kids come home from
school they've caught the dreaded 'nits'

They've implemented cut-backs and got
rid of 'Nitty Norah'
You're now an entomologist, an expert
bug explorer
You thought that you'd been vigilant, they
really are a bitch
You tremble at the thought of them and
frantically itch

The females are like whores and they lay
many eggs a day
They take on several lovers and then lead
the males astray
Jumping in and out of heads, they're little
more than hookers
A curse upon our children's hair the evil
mother suckers

(Cont ...)

High-tech fancy lotions, you don't care
about the cost
These vile, malicious creatures could
survive a holocaust
Despite the electronic comb they're very
much alive
They're dancing in the tea tree oil and
doing a high-five

You fumigate and sanitise and
decontaminate
You might as well burn down the house
and quickly relocate
So if you think you're rid of them well
bloomin' well think twice
At last you've sorted out the kids but
now *you've* got head lice!

Your Mum's an Expert Spy

As many of you will be aware, I visit schools to give poetry workshops. I wrote this poem to entertain the children. It always receives a positive response and mums definitely relate to this one too.

Your Mum's an Expert Spy

She knows just how you did it and she
knows just where you were
Don't try to hide the evidence, there's
nothing gets past her
Don't have a go at fooling her and don't
attempt to lie
Deception is just pointless 'cos your
mum's an expert spy

Do not rely on Google or depend on
social media
'Cos if you've got a mum you've got your
own encyclopedia
She knows just who your friends are and
she'll tell you if they're bad
She knows just when you're happy and
you can't hide when you're sad

She'll help you out of trouble and be there
at any cost
Unless your mum can't find it, is it really
even lost?
Whatever you may ask about, your mum
will know the score
Your mum thinks she knows
everything…but nan knows even more!

Something to Chew On
(A collection of thought-provoking poems)

Stand Up to Bullying

I usually visit schools during Anti-Bullying Week. I wrote this poem to read to the children in both primary and secondary schools. It often inspires them to write on this subject during poetry workshops and some of the poetry they've written has been both heartwarming and heartbreaking. Of course, bullying isn't exclusive to schools or children, it takes place in all walks of life. I'd like to think that if anyone witnessed bullying, they'd both defend and support the victim. After all, nobody knows when they might be the victim themselves.

Stand Up to Bullying

Pulling someone down will never help
you be the best
The ones you think admire you truly fail
to be impressed
Meanness is a weakness, you may think
you feel empowered
Breaking someone else will show the
world that you're a coward

Confidence is silent, insecurity is loud
There's nothing brave in joining an
intimidating crowd
If you think it's big to make a person feel
so small
Remember that next week it could be
you against the wall

The actions of a bully leave us terrified
and sore
The silence of our friends will traumatise
us even more
If you see injustice don't be scared to use
your voice
Listen to your conscience and accept you
have a choice

(Cont...)

They say there's strength in numbers, I
believe this to be true
There's fewer bullies in this world than
folk like me and you
Show them solidarity is what it's all about
Together we can find the nerve to call
that bully out

You can't be friends with everyone but be
a friend to all
Should someone be pushed over always
be there if they fall
When they're lying in a grave regrets are
much too late
Because you looked the other way and
helped to seal their fate

Invisible, Unseen, Unknown

*It's tragic that in the 21st century people
are homeless. I don't believe anyone
would choose to sleep on the streets,
particularly in the dead of winter.
Whatever the tragic circumstances
that have led to someone being in this
situation, we should all show compassion
and avoid being judgemental. I have
a very dear friend that I've known
from my school days called Teresa who
works tirelessly and selflessly to help the
homeless. I'm always very humbled by
the number of good people like Teresa
who help those in this desperate situation.
If only our governments throughout the
world were full of Teresas.*

Invisible, Unseen, Unknown

Scorned and spat on, robbed and beaten
Haven't washed and haven't eaten
Wandering, frozen to the bone
Invisible, unseen, unknown

Cold hard pavements, cold hard facts
All they own rests on their backs
A twist of fate, a life event
They lost their job, can't pay the rent

Austerity and welfare cuts
A national shame, no ifs no buts
A runaway too scared to sleep
Addicted child too numb to weep

Sleeping rough in makeshift beds
Try to rest their weary heads
Passing revellers celebrate
Step over them to urinate

And all around prosperity
Is flaunted with vulgarity
The great divide, the truth laid bare
But those that matter just don't care

Life is just a game of chance
A victim of a circumstance
You just might find yourself alone
invisible, unseen, unknown

Let's Kick Cancer's Arse!

Last year I entered a competition to write a poem for 'Relay for Life', a cancer charity. I was delighted to win. I was asked to read the poem at our National Stadium at the annual Relay for Life Event but unfortunately I was out of the country at the time. Thankfully, my lovely friend Becky, herself a cancer survivor, kindly agreed to read the poem for me at the event. I must say she did it proud. I'm willing to bet that all of you either know someone who's survived cancer, know someone who's died of cancer or even had cancer yourself. I only hope the day will come when a cure is found for this horrible disease and we can then kick cancer's arse!

Let's Kick Cancer's Arse!

You're a life that's cut short by a deadline
While you viciously spread day-by-day
Like a coward you watch from the
sideline
As you're taking our loved ones away

But cancer's a word not a sentence
Be assured that we're on the attack
While you shamelessly show no
repentance
We are finding the strength to fight back

A crayon still colours when broken
You miscalculate how we can cope
So beware of the force you've awoken
There's no medicine better than hope

We are more than a worthy contender
We intend to ensure your defeat
So no more on our knees we surrender
We defiantly rise to our feet

So cancer you started this contest
It's a matter of time till you're licked
We'll rejoice on the day of your inquest
When they tell us your arse has been
kicked!

I'm Still Here

Alzheimer's and Dementia are devastating diseases that have touched the lives of many. My own dear father-in-law died a couple of years ago, his last few years blighted by the torture of this horrible disease. RIP Ernest, you were the best father-in-law a girl could have had. I will remember you as the kind, thoughtful, intelligent and extremely talented man you were.

I'm Still Here

Like a hidden monster, seed sown in
my DNA
Confused and disconnected, life
unravels day-by-day
The face that's in the mirror looks
familiar yet unclear
You may think that I'm far away but I
know I'm still here

My character's been washed away like
footprints on the sand
A cognitive return to birth that fate has
cruelly planned
Disease has locked the door and simply
thrown away the key
My cerebral decline conspires to then
imprison me

I tell the same old stories, to remind
me of my past
To reassure me who I am, my world is
fading fast
My repetitious mutterings may seem
inconsequential
They're refuge from the chaos,
understand that they're essential

(Cont...)

So be my co-conspirator, to help
maintain normality
Have patience with the tedium, enduring
the banality
Sing with me the songs that for a lifetime
I've enjoyed
Help unlock the part of me that cannot
be destroyed

Your kindness is a comfort as I face my
long goodbye
Remember me the way I was, don't let
me see you cry
Love, respect and dignity will help me
face my fear
Hold my hand, be there for me, while
ever I'm still here

Dunblane

On 13th March 1996 a gunman entered a school in Dunblane in Scotland. He shot and killed 16 children, fifteen of them aged 5 and one of them aged 6, and their 45 year old teacher, before killing himself. I refuse to mention his name. I wrote this poem in remembrance of the children and their teacher who lost their lives that tragic day.

Dunblane

When buds awaken from their sleep
Whilst banishing the morning frost
We think of them and gently weep
Reflecting on those childhoods lost

Each story ended at the start
Their hopes and dreams left lying there
As lives were cruelly torn apart
Where once they'd played without a care

A teacher left to face her fear
Protecting them at any cost
Remembering with every tear
The day that innocence was lost

The world stood still, a nation grieved
The pain and horror still remain
Humanity – betrayed, deceived
That spring time morning in Dunblane

Another Day, Another Grave

Following the Dunblane massacre, the Conservative government of John Major introduced the Firearms (Amendment) Act 1997, which banned all cartridge ammunition handguns with the exception of .22 calibre single-shot weapons in England, Scotland and Wales. Following the 1997 General Election, the Labour government of Tony Blair introduced the Firearms (Amendment) (No. 2) Act 1997, banning the remaining .22 cartridge handgun. Unfortunately there are still shooting incidents and particularly in the USA. Here's a poem I wrote on this subject.

Another Day, Another Grave

Headline news, a minute's silence
Carnage, bloodshed, shocking violence
Platitudes that seem grotesque
A lifeless child beneath a desk

They pay the price but life is cheap
Some 'pray for them' whilst others weep
Someone's daughter, someone's son…
And someone's child that fired the gun

Nations grieve and lives are shattered
'Bearing arms' was all that mattered
Drive by shootings, homicides
Killing sprees and suicides

They count the cost, ignore the cause
Oppose amendments to the laws
'Land of the free, home of the brave'
Another day, another grave…

Bloody Sunday

On 30th January 1972, the parachute regiment of the British Army shot 26 unarmed civilians during a civil rights march in Derry, Northern Ireland. Thirteen were killed immediately and another one died a few months later. Bloody Sunday came to be regarded as one of the most significant events of the Troubles, because many civilians were killed by forces of the state, in full view of the public and the press. In 2010, following the Savile Inquiry, the then Prime Minister, David Cameron stated "There is no doubt, there is nothing equivocal, there are no ambiguities. What happened on Bloody Sunday was both unjustified and unjustifiable. It was wrong".

Bloody Sunday

Down Rossville Street they made their
way
To meet their friends that fateful day
To ask the world to hear their voice
They had no rights – they had no choice

Men imprisoned without trial
The climate cold, the mood was vile
They marched in peace – no bombs, no
guns
Mothers, daughters, fathers, sons

The British Army lay in wait
Led by orders from the state
They opened fire and shot them down
A massacre that shamed the Crown

Friends and family, weeping, pleading
As their loved ones lay there bleeding
Monstrous, cruel, grotesque attack
They even shot them in the back

Fourteen people lost their lives
Leaving children, mothers, wives
Haunted by their dying screams
Some were only in their teens

(Cont...)

The streets were soaked with blood in
Derry
Tortured souls had kin to bury
But still no sign of charity
No guilt for the barbarity

Repugnant lies, bare faced collusion
Fuelled the hate and disillusion
Terror, carnage, more blood spilled
Thousands wounded, thousands killed

Decades passed the truth denied
Still the state and army lied
But when the day of justice came
They had to hang their heads in shame

The years have passed, they've worked
for peace
For war and bombs, bad blood to cease
Together they must have a voice
To earn their rights and have a choice

The Great Hunger

The Great Hunger was a period of mass starvation and disease in Ireland between 1845 and 1849. It's often referred to, mostly outside Ireland, as the 'Irish Famine'.
Due to ethnic prejudice, oppression and mass evictions, approximately one million died and a further two million emigrated whilst food was exported as they starved.
In British India, during the years 1876-79, famine claimed the lives of between six and ten million people. Between 1896 and 1902, an almost certainly even higher toll from starvation and disease (the estimates range from six to nineteen million) was recorded there, just as the reign of Victoria, the Empress-Queen, came to its close.

The Great Hunger

In 1845 when times were prospering in
'Blighty'
Industrial revolution built an empire rich
and mighty
Under British rule the Irish suffered
deprivation
Subjected to a system of oppression and
starvation

The penal laws denied the vote, forbade
an education
Seizing land and property, inflicting
degradation
Subsisting on their rented farms as little
more than slaves
Then brutally discarded in their wretched,
unmarked graves

Trevelyan's ambivalence made sure that
aid was thwarted
He ordered corn and cattle to be
shamefully exported
Refusing intervention, diabolically
observing
Declaring that the Irish were depraved
and undeserving

(Cont...)

To starve where food was plentiful, a
sickening disaster
Treated with dispassion by their heartless
English master
The Hague Convention states that it must
never be denied
Such willful, ruthless massacre an act of
genocide

A quarter of the populace were killed or
forced to leave
Impassive to their suffering, a nation left
to grieve
Their fight for independence brought
hostility from some
These strong, resilient people still believe
their day will come

Beyond the Wall

*Here's a poem I've written to raise
awareness of the terrible plight of those
unfortunate women and children
subjected to a life of rape, torture and
sometimes death in the industrial schools
run by the Christian Brothers and the
'Magadelene' laundries run by nuns.
During the visit of Pope Francis to Dublin
in August 2018, many people displayed
this poem in the windows along the
route of his journey and even posted it
on the doors of Catholic churches and
establishments. Fortunately, Ireland is
a very different country today but it is
important to remember and recognise
the suffering of those poor women and
children.*

Beyond the Wall

Vulnerable, abandoned, godforsaken and
neglected
Impoverished, unfortunate and cruelly
unprotected
The world outside oblivious, did no-one
care at all?
Indifferent to the wretched stolen lives
beyond the wall

Children raped and beaten and
methodically brutalised
Sadistic violence commonplace but how
come no-one realised?
Fatal beatings certified as accidental
death
Impartial to their suffering, no point in
wasting breath

A child who was a 'runner' could expect
a Brother's fist
Battered with the hurley stick, a broken
leg or wrist
Dragged back to their torment, locked
behind the iron gates
A neverending nightmare, only dreaded
hell awaits

(Cont...)

The mentally defective, wanton women,
'whores' and 'prostitutes'
Pregnant out of wedlock, adolescent girls
and destitutes
Oppression, degradation and a system
that was punitive
The selling of their babies, diabolically
lucrative

Toiling in the laundries, they were little
more than slaves
Worked to death then cruelly cast aside
in unmarked graves
A daily dose of silence, prayer and gross
humiliation
Spartan, cold, indefinite, their bleak
incarceration

Alcohol and drug abuse, and mindless
criminality
Help to numb the memory of terror and
brutality
Misfits of society, they fight their private
war
Shamefully betrayed absurdly locked
away once more

Lies, deceit, conspiracies to cover up the
truth
Wicked clerics free to rape and violate
our youth
The Pope is in denial does he just not
care at all?
Indifferent to those wretched stolen lives
beyond the wall

An Irish Ballad

I may not be Oscar Wilde, George Bernard Shaw or James Joyce but I'm still a poet inspired by Ireland.

An Irish Ballad

Where the wind sings as it rushes
Over lush, verdant pastures of green
Roaming through foliage and bushes
Taking rest in a welcome *shebeen

I drank in the folklore and history
And dined on the musical fare
Enchanted by tales of great mystery
Enraptured as mirth filled the air

The Irish – beguiling and charming
Will greet you with warmth and great
cheer
The lilt of their voices disarming
As melodic sweet sounds filled my ear

Leprechauns danced in the twilight
Observing the moon rising high
Casting their spells in the half-light
Giving way to a velvety sky

(Cont...)

I awoke the next morn as the sun rose
And the tall grass was kissed by the dew
Gently I trod through the meadows
Where a blanket of fresh shamrocks grew

She's a rainbow that's drawn to perfection
On a breathtaking daydream blue sky
I may speak of her with great affection
She's my family, my Ireland, that's why

*shebeen (line four) is an unlicensed
establishment or private house selling
alcohol and typically regarded as slightly
disreputable

Magnificent Mayo

*What better way to celebrate my
ancestral home, the magical county
of Mayo on the west coast of Ireland,
than with a poem. It's a place that
would inspire any poet to write
lyrical literature.*

Magnificent Mayo

My eyes roam freely cross verdant valleys
and rolling hills of green
The fertile foothills of craggy mountains,
the air so fresh and clean
I wander through rambling pastures, to
the coast of Killala Bay
In the wonderful county of Mayo on the
Wild Atlantic Way

A county of myths and great legends and
tales of the Pirate Queen
Home of McBride and of Davitt, the boys
of the red and green
The breathtaking island of Achill, its cliffs
tumbling down to the sea
Unspoiled, enchanting, beguiling,
conspiring to captivate me

Castlebar, Foxford, Belmullet, Ballycastle
and Ballina
The picturesque town of Westport, the
charisma of Matt Molloy's Bar
Scaling the heights of Croagh Patrick,
where the clouds kiss the Heavens above
My ancestral county of Mayo, this
magnificent place that I love

Magical Maughold

In 2007 my husband, Michael, daughter,
Jessica and I relocated from 'God's Own
County' – Yorkshire, to the Isle of Man.
We settled in a small village in the north
called Maughold (pronounced Mack-old).
Not a day goes by that I don't pinch myself.
It truly is a beautiful and magical place.
Here's my tribute to Maughold

Magical Maughold

A luxurious patchwork of pastures of
green
'Neath a silvery blanket of mist
Such breathtaking beauty, a wondrous
scene
It's a place surely Heaven has kissed

I climbed Maughold Head as the morning
sun rose
And the darkness surrendered to light
Where the buttery bloom of the golden
gorse grows
And adventurous seabirds take flight

Wispy white clouds on forget-me-not skies
Seem to blush in the warmth of the sun
A chorus of birds sing a morning reprise
As if forming a choir one by one

The waves gently lap at the craggy
coastline
As the sea wears the sun like a jewel
Like diamonds that sparkle beneath the
sunshine
Looking over towards North Barrule

The village lies tranquil, unspoiled and
serene
A perfectly drawn picture-postcard
I stop for a moment to drink in the scene
As I quietly tread through the churchyard

(Cont...)

Oh beautiful Maughold a feast for my eyes
Changing your mood without reason
From warm, sun-kissed rainbows to dark
stormy skies
Replacing your clothes with each season

A vivid blue carpet in Ballaglass Glen
Where the bluebells spread under the
trees
Dancing to welcome the springtime again
As if choreographed by the breeze

A canvas of colours fades into the night
As the sun turns the sea liquid-gold
The stars, glowing embers, appear at
twilight
A magnificent sight to behold

There's things that are priceless in life they
say
Their value is way beyond worth
I hope I'll live here 'till my dying day
It's my own piece of Heaven on Earth

Royal Ramsey

Four miles north of Maughold, is the 'capital of the north', Ramsey. It's often referred to as 'Royal Ramsey' because of a famous visit by Queen Victoria and Prince Albert. When I venture down south and travel back across Snaefell Mountain, I never tire of the magnificent view of Ramsey, the jewel of the north, shining by the sea as I approach the descent into this wonderful little town on my way home to Maughold. There's a saying on the Isle of Man "it's always sunny in Ramsey". It's true. It's often raining and cloudy elsewhere but it's very rare that the sun isn't shining in Ramsey.

Royal Ramsey

'Neath the slumbering giant of North
Barrule
Where the sweet smell of heather roams
free
The gem of the north, an exquisite jewel
Resplendent it shines by the sea

The sun scatters sequins across the still lake
As the wild flowers nod in the breeze
The picturesque Mooragh your breath it
will take
As the wind lightly drifts through the trees

Stopping to chat down on Parliament Street
The town's steady, strong beating heart
Familiar faces just happen to meet
A place for new friendships to start

I pass by the harbour to stroll to the bay
For a taste of the salty sea air
The wind nudges gently the boats as they
sway
As it blows the loose strands of my hair

(Cont...)

A fringe of white lace is caressing the sand
As the waves slowly roll in the bay
A place where young lovers can walk hand
in hand
Where they dream that their children will
play

To walk by the sea wall and drink in the
view
With the warm summer sun on my face
A piece of perfection, the sky painted blue
How I love this magnificent place

Majestically rising the old iron pier
Many childhoods etched into its beams
Sweet summer memories of yesteryear
Now a beacon of hope and new dreams

So if I grow old on this beautiful isle
I'll pass by this spot every day
To feast on the beauty and rest for a while
Looking out over Ramsey's south bay

My Wakefield Childhood

We all love a bit of nostalgia and I hope you'll enjoy reading this next poem. If you're from the Wakefield area, I'm sure you'll recognise many, if not all of the familiar landmarks. Even if you're not, I'm sure you'll relate to many of the childhood references, especially if you're of a certain age.

My Wakefield Childhood

The place where I grew up became a place I
left behind
The playground of my youth is firmly
etched upon my mind
Our bodies grew, our minds did too, we
lost touch with our mates
But remnants of our childhoods still
remain on those estates

At Parkhill Pit we played amongst the
heaps of coal and slack
Our mothers had a job to clean us up when
we got back
What a sight, we were 'black bright' we'd
surely be in trouble
They pulled down all the prefabs and we
played between the rubble

Dandelion and Burdock was our favourite
Ben Shaws pop
We always took the empties back to old
McKenna's shop
Packs of *Spangles*, sweetie bangles, *Black
Jacks*, penny chews
Extra money for our treats, the bottles were
re-used

On Saturday we'd watch the *Wacky Races*
on TV
We went down to the cinema – then known
as *ABC*
We'd watch cartoons, then afternoons we'd
still be playing out

(Cont...)

Or take a trip to *Sun Lane Baths* and have a
splash about

The mini train in Wakey Park amongst our
special treats
We'd call in to the *Bon Bon* for an ice-
cream and some sweets
Climbing trees and scraping knees, we
cherished simple things
Even Wakey Market had a roundabout and
swings!

There was a thriving market and the shops
were booming too
Miss Siama, Avaganda even *Oobidoo*
A cheesecloth shirt, a denim skirt, some
flares from *C&A*
The *Record Bar* in Kirkgate sold the music
of the day

At weekends in our teens we'd have a dance
down at the *Mecca*
We'd catch the bus to Wakey on a worn out
double decker
Under the clock, in our best frock we'd
gather in the station
And do the 'Westgate Run' before we
reached our destination

And now I'm in my fifties I look back upon
those times
Sitting on the 'causey edge' and singing
childish rhymes
Skipping ropes and dreams and hopes that
sometimes fell apart
The place where I grew up forever etched
upon my heart

Something Sweet
(A collection of poems to warm the heart)

The Magic of Books

I originally wrote this to read to the children on my visits to the local schools but it has proved popular with both adults and children alike. Who doesn't enjoy escaping every day life by reading a good book?

The Magic of Books

A book is a dream you can hold in your hand
It can whisk you away to a faraway land
Magical stories, adventures to share
Travel the world without leaving your chair

Open a book and you'll open your mind
Turning each page there are legends to find
Mermaids and unicorns, wizards and spies
Mythical creatures in every disguise

New friends to meet simply waiting inside
Daring to dream with your eyes open wide
Live a whole lifetime in one afternoon
Step back in time, even fly to the moon

The more you read, the more you'll know
The more you know, the further you'll go
A story book world filled with all you need
Anything's possible when you can read!

What Christmas Means to Me

Last Christmas (2019) I was asked by one of the primary schools on the island to write a poem for the children to perform at their Christmas concert. I was delighted to be able to write this poem for them and they certainly did it justice with their fantastic performance. Well done Bunscoill Rhumsaa in Ramsey!

What Christmas Means to Me

Putting on our Christmas sweaters
Making lists and writing letters
Helping mum to trim the tree
That's what Christmas means to me

As the festive season starts
Welcome friends with open hearts
Being as good as we can be
That's what Christmas means to me

Carol singers, Christmas lights
New pyjamas, cosy nights
Stories on my grandma's knee
That's what Christmas means to me

Here comes Santa on his sleigh
Bringing gifts on Christmas Day
Flying high across the sea
That's what Christmas means to me

Lots of fun and festive cheer
No more school until next year!
More cold turkey for our tea
That's what Christmas means to me

As the festive season ends
Spent with family and friends
The greatest gifts are always free
That's what Christmas means to me

Let's Hear it for the Boys!

If you bought my book Sugar and Spice – a collection of poetry relating to all things female, you may remember a poem in that book entitled 'A Woman's World' that I performed on Channel 5's The Wright Stuff. Well, let's not forget the contribution that the male species make to this world. They're often expected to conform to certain stereotypes so I wrote this to celebrate all kinds of men.

Let's Hear it for the Boys!

They say a good man's hard to find but I
don't think that's true
We shouldn't underestimate the things
that they can do
A man can grow a beard and coolly
hide his double chin
Decide to have a buzzcut if his hair is
getting thin

They come in all varieties, in every
shape and size
But is it right to criticise him if a grown
man cries?
At work they're often told to wear a
collar and a shirt
But really does it matter if they
sometimes wear a skirt?

I wouldn't want to be a man, I think
they have it rough
They're educated to be strong, expected
to be tough
So now's the time to celebrate and really
make some noise
We couldn't live without them so let's
hear it for the boys!

From the Cradle to the Grave

This next poem was written in early July 2018 to celebrate seventy years of the NHS. Little did I know that a week later I'd fall and end up in hospital! I'll never take for granted our wonderful NHS.

From the Cradle to the Grave

Darkness in a post-war nation NHS a
true salvation
Will save you at your very worst
And hold you as you breathe your first

Attending to the frail and ill
Providing vaccines and the pill
From the cradle to the grave
A vision that was truly brave

Things that money could not buy
Reasurrance as you cry
A cup of tea, a friendly smile
Prepared to go the extra mile

An institution set apart
Our country's constant beating heart
A promise to remain steadfast
And hold you as you breathe your last

Truth

Last year (2019) the theme of National Poetry Day was 'Truth'. Here's a poem I wrote to celebrate.

Truth

Slapped by the truth – kissed with a lie?
Be honest or misleading?
The truth will often make you cry
But lies can leave you bleeding

The naked truth, it's my belief
Defeats the best dressed lie
Which often offers quick relief
Then leaves you high and dry

The facts remain the same
But they will often be denied
No matter what you claim
The truth will be identified

So tell the truth, don't live a lie
And soon enough you'll see
Honest men can verify
The truth will set you free

The Parish Walk

The annual Parish Walk on the Isle of Man takes place on the third weekend of June. Competitors walk 85 miles around the island, covering all parishes. They have to complete the course within 24 hours. It's no mean feat. I enjoy walking myself but can't imagine the training, dedication and stamina it takes to take part in, let alone complete, the Parish Walk. Here's a tribute to all those brave 'Parish Walkers'.

The Parish Walk

At eight o'clock they're on their way
And start the race without delay
The Parish Walkers dare to tread
Where many feet before have bled

Head to Braddan with conviction
Reach Marown without much friction
Now they're feeling motivated
Making sure to stay hydrated

Santon – they're all in their step
Inspired by the months of prep
In Malew there's a few folk flagging
By Arbory they've started lagging

Up through Rushen, some start
dropping
Others wouldn't dream of stopping
Doing well against the clock
Until they reach the dreaded Sloc

Patrick next then onto Peel
The competition's getting real
Whilst some stop off to urinate
Their feet are in a right old state

Kirk Michael - now they're feeling
rough
And some have clearly had enough
Ballaugh - they really feel the strain
But head to Jurby through the pain

(Cont...)

Reaching Bride they have a snack
Their toenails slowly turning black
Supporters keep them in the zone
At least they'll never walk alone

Andreas then through Lezayre
Ramsey, into Parliament Square
On the coast road, feeling drained
Hips and calves are feeling pained

In Maughold there's a welcome scene
The barbie on the village green
They're serving burgers, cakes and teas
By now they're nearly on their knees

With less than twenty miles to go
The blisters burning every toe
They dream about a nice warm bath
And head along the coast road path

At Lonan every muscle's sore
Almost there, there's not much more
Then into Onchan, through Port Jack
And down the prom, no looking back

The finish line is in their sight
Triumphant in the morning light
They've sweated blood and tasted fear
They'll do it all again next year!

A Bittersweet Affair
(A collection of poems inspired by
the Covid-19 pandemic of 2020)

Stay at Home

Back in March 2020, when countries began to lockdown due to the corona virus, we were all told to 'Stay at Home'. Some found this more difficult than others. Some understandably struggled with the loneliness and became anxious about the isolation and uncertainty of the situation. Meanwhile, the frontline staff had to put those fears aside for the good of society and bravely put their lives at risk to save our lives.

Stay at Home

We live with the uncertainty our world
has been disrupted
Our lives have been turned upside
down and swiftly interrupted
And now we're told to stay at home and
some have had enough
They want the right to go outside – they
think they've got it tough

But…

Terrified and traumatised, some risk
their lives each day
They hold onto a stranger's hand and
watch them pass away
Collapsing in the corridor, they put
aside their strife
They shake it off, then dry their tears
and save another life

And…

As we stay at home we've had to cancel
all our plans
We're missing time with family, our
grandkids and our grans
We're stuck at home in lockdown, we
can't go out with our friends
There's only Skype and FaceTime till
this dreadful nightmare ends

(Cont...)

But…

If our loved one's dying we can't be
there at their side
A medic has to break the news that they
have sadly died
The nurses tried to comfort them, they
stroked their hair and smiled
We couldn't hold our precious gran or
even worse our child

So…

Those defying lockdown, let them stop
and think again
Of those who've sacrificed their lives,
brave women and brave men
They put aside their doubts and fears,
faced countless threats and dangers
They died leaving their loved ones as
they saved the lives of strangers

And…

Still their colleagues forge ahead, their
hands are cracked and sore
Exhausted and at breaking point they
carry on once more
The fear in every patient's eyes, the
hacking, gasping cough
The click of life support machines each
time that they're switched off

(Cont...)

So…

As the world applauds them around
8.00 p.m. each Thursday
There's just no point in joining them if
you go out on Friday
The message is quite clear to those who
are inclined to roam
The only way to beat this beast is if we
stay at home!

The Year the World Was Paused

As a result of the pandemic, many of us have been able to spend time at home with our families, discovered the countryside and enjoyed becoming more active. During lockdown pollution was greatly reduced and many people found they enjoyed working from home. Quite a few of them continue to do so. This year, the world was paused and we had the time to contemplate about what is really important. I hope you learned ways to change your lives for the better because I know I certainly did. This was also a winning poem in this year's Poetry Trail during Manx Litfest.

The Year the World Was Paused

In the spring of 2020, the world came
to a halt
Our lives were changed forever, we were
reset to default
Pubs and schools were empty, life came
to a standstill
We had the opportunity to jump right
off the treadmill

Those left on the frontline, once so truly
underrated
Now they're worth their weight in gold,
at last appreciated
Posties, farmers, bobbies, binmen, shop
staff, teachers too
NHS and scientists, all help us to pull
through

And those of us who stay at home to do
as we've been told
Have had the time to contemplate as
life's been put on hold
To cherish simple pleasures, the
blackbirds as they sing
A world free from pollution and the
warmth of early spring

(Cont...)

We haven't missed designer clothes or
driving flashy cars
Or wasting time in coffee shops,
expensive, fancy bars
We miss our friends and relatives, the
ones who make us smile
We'd love to see them face-to-face and
visit for a while

Making art and music whilst we're in
captivity
Enjoying time to delve into our
creativity
At last free from the shackles of those
everyday demands
Encouraging our children as they use
their little hands

We have the chance to change our lives,
the way we now exist
A golden opportunity and one that can't
be missed
A brand new way of living that this
deadly virus caused
A positive reaction to the year the world
was paused...

Quarantine Quandaries

In times of adversity, we often turn to humour to help us cope. Many little luxuries were denied to us during the lockdown phase of the pandemic. I made a video of this poem and I must say when I watch it back now I do wonder how I dared to be seen on the world wide web with my hair in such a state! Here's a humorous take on life in quarantine.

Quarantine Quandaries

I'm in week nine of lockdown and I
think I'm going mad
My living room – gatecrashed by Zoom
Another crackpot fad

We look just like the Brady Bunch in
squares across the screen
And sure enough, I look quite rough
Locked up in quarantine

Now things are getting ugly and I'm
missing my beautician
My facial hair makes me despair
I need a damned magician
I'll have to get my razor out to try to
save my marriage
Hoist up my boobs and trim my pubes
And shave my undercarriage

I think I'll be like Britney and I'll shave
off all my hair
I have to cringe I've chopped my fringe
It's now beyond repair
I'm piling on the timber and I'm getting
far too big
I will no doubt end up with gout
I'm eating like a pig

(Cont...)

I'm living in my trackies 'cos I can't fit in
my dress
My camel toe is there on show
I look a proper mess
I thought I'd take up running but it just
made me perspire
The exercise, it rubbed my thighs
And set my bush on fire

I've tried to social distance but the park
is full of joggers
The rules now state to meet one mate
It's gone down well with doggers
The whole thing was avoidable, there's
no denying that
What caused this state? Some wazzock
ate a dirty chuffing bat!

Isolation Revelation

As the lockdown phase continued many aspects were a source of humour for me. It never ceased to amaze me how different people responded to the situation and from the comfort of my armchair I enjoyed observing how everyone else was coping. I must say I witnessed some pretty bizarre behaviour at times!

Isolation Revelation

This new year she really had high hopes
of things to come
But now it's May, to her dismay
She's nowt to wipe her bum

She's living in a nightmare and it's gone
from bad to worse
She's terrified to step outside
This virus is a curse

She's standing by her window and her
curtains start to twitch
'Cos number ten went out again
She feels she ought to snitch

He wasn't one for exercise but now he
runs each day
He leaves the house, avoids his spouse
It's pretty fair to say

The one at Number forty-two now
thinks she's Mary Berry
She's no great shakes 'cos as she bakes
She's knocking back the sherry

Her husband's stuck inside and he can't
meet his concubine
He's had a fling with some young thing
From number twenty-nine

(Cont...)

But she's got seven kids and they've
been training with Joe Wicks
He's fixed her core and pelvic floor
She's learned a few new tricks

Her kids don't wear a mask outside –
she really does despair
They pick up worms and lots of germs
They just don't seem to a care

They wipe 'em on their jumpers if they
think their hands are manky
And just in case, mum cleans their face
By spitting on her hanky

They all go out on Thursday night, it
started off just clapping
They're out of hand – they've formed a
band
Now little Johnny's rapping

If they don't keep their distance she'll
just tell them to back off
She'll then attack with anti-bac
If they should dare to cough

She caught her husband sneaking out,
the dirty rotten swine
He's servicing that cheap young thing
At number twenty-nine

(Cont...)

She told him he could not come back,
she really went ballistic
The filthy beast is now deceased
Another sad statistic

She told him that it wasn't right for
them to socialise
But he went out and dared to flout
And didn't sanitise

She's joined an online dating app for
warmth and reassurance
When this thing ends, her new
boyfriends
Will spend his life insurance!

Blue Poppies

The following poem was inspired by a painting by my daughter, Jessica. I wrote this poem in remembrance of those frontline workers who died serving their community and saving the lives of those suffering from Covid-19. We are forever indebted to them, lest we forget.

Blue Poppies

Parades of poppies vivid blue
Tenacious blooms of vibrant hue
Whose chiffon petals gently wave
And kiss the soil upon your grave

Trustworthy and reliable
Devotion undeniable
A selflessness unique and rare
A promise to protect and care

So steadfast in your loyalty
Whilst serving your community
Heroically you wiped your tears
Benevolently hid your fears

Blue poppies resting in the shade
Recall the sacrifice you made
A symbol of the people's debt
Forevermore lest we forget

A letter from the author...

Thank you so much for taking the time to read *A Variety of Verse*. I do hope you enjoyed it.

It's been nearly two years since I published my first three poetry books. I can hardly believe it's been less than five years since I regularly started writing poetry again. In that time I've enjoyed so many great poetry-related experiences. I've met numerous interesting people, including poets, writers and, of course, followers who read my poetry.

Since my last books were published, I've started going into schools to give poetry workshops. This has given me huge pleasure and I hope it has inspired some children to write their own poetry, not just during my visits, but afterwards too. I'm very grateful to the teachers and staff at the schools who warmly welcome me and to the children who engage so readily and enthusiastically.

(Cont...)

I've also been given a regular poetry slot on Manx Radio's *Late Lunch*. The presenters of the show have been so kind and encouraging, particularly Christy DeHaven, Beth Espey and Howard Caine. We even recorded a two hour show from my home entitled 'Christmas at Carol's' which was broadcast on Christmas Day 2019 in the afternoon with Christy, Beth, Howard and their colleague Ben Hartley.

Of course the very best thing about publishing a book is getting a response from you, the reader. I've been delighted with the response I've had over the last couple of years. I keep in touch with many of you on a daily basis through Facebook, Instagram and Twitter. Since September 2019 I've been writing a two-line rhyming couplet and posting it every day across all my social media platforms. These are *Mrs Yorkshire's Words of Wit and Wisdom* and they've proved a huge success. Many of you check in daily to read them and leave comments. I've been privileged to build up a great relationship with you. Your comments really do make it so worthwhile and encourage me to write more.

(Cont...)

A book containing hundreds of my words of wit and wisdom will be available very soon, I hope you'll enjoy reading it.

I'll also be releasing a special edition of festive words of wit and wisdom in time for Christmas 2020.

All my books are available to purchase on Amazon and in all book shops. If you can't see the book on the shelf, just ask the shop assistant who will be happy to order it in for you.

I love to know what you think about my books so please feel free to tweet me, or leave me a message on Instagram or Facebook. All authors love getting reviews and I'm no exception. I'd love you to leave me a review on Amazon.

If I'm out and about performing, please come and say hello.

You can write to me at Red Lizard Ltd, PO Box 18, Ramsey, Isle of Man, IM99 4PG or e-mail me at carolellis2012@gmail.com

(Cont...)

I'm happy to perform at corporate and charity events, social functions and engage in TV and radio appearances.

Thank you again for reading this book and for your continued support. I'm writing all the time and look forward to publishing more in the future.

Here's to more great times and great rhymes!

Carol Ellis

Mrs Yorkshire the Baking Bard

X

Visiting Bunscoill Rhumsaa, Ramsey, Isle of Man to give a poetry workshop to the junior school children.

Performing at the annual Manx Litfest
event.

The launch of the *Late Lunch* afternoon show on Manx Radio.

With Christy DeHaven (left) and Beth
Espey (right), the presenters of Manx
Radio's *Late Lunch*. Mrs Yorkshire always
brings cake when she's on the radio!

With husband Michael – 'Mr Yorkshire'
(standing), and Manx Radio presenters
Christy DeHaven, Ben Hartley, Beth
Espey and Howard Caine, recording a
special show from 'The Maughold Arms'
(the pub in Mrs Yorkshire's house!) for
Christmas Day 2019.

Visiting King William's College,
Castletown, Isle of Man during Anti-
Bullying Week for a poetry workshop. The
children are holding copies of a pocket-
sized, laminated leaflet with the poems
Stand Up to Bullying and *Be Kind* printed
on either side.

Reading a winning poem at the launch of the
Isle of Man Poetry Society's annual Poetry
Trail.

Visiting the Isle of Man's Hospice,
Douglas to perform poetry.

Performing at a charity event in Onchan, Isle of Man with the Platform Theatre Group.

Performing at one of the regular, very popular Open Mic events in Douglas, Isle of Man, organised by Hazel Teare, a well-respected and talented Manx poet.

Visiting Chris Payne, Managing Director
of Effort-Free Media Ltd who helps
consultants, trainers and coaches to create
quality e-products and who assisted in
the publication of the trilogy of poetry
books, *A Slice of Humour, Food for
Thought* and *Sugar and Spice* in 2018.
Chris continues to be an inspiration and a
good friend.

Visiting Manx Radio in Douglas for one
of her regular slots on the afternoon show
Late Lunch.

In Dublin, Ireland, with the statue of poet
and playwright Oscar Wilde (1854-1900).

In Portugal with a statue of famous
Portuguese poet João Braz (1912-1993)

A guest at the Christmas Concert of the Bunscoill Rhumsaa, Ramsey, Isle of Man, where the children performed a poem written for their concert entitled *What Christmas Means to Me.*

Performing at the 50th birthday party of her friend, Carol Sutcliffe. A poem was written especially for the occasion.

With Manx Radio presenters Beth Espey
(left) and Christy DeHaven (right) on one
of her regular visits to the radio station.

Performing the poem *A Woman's World* on Channel 5's *The Wright Stuff* for International Women's Day.

Performing a poem specially written for the wonderful Matthew Wright on his very last day on Channel 5's *The Wright Stuff* after eighteen years of presenting the show. There'll never be another presenter like Matthew on TV!

Some of the wonderful poems written by
the children of Ballaugh School, Ballaugh,
Isle of Man during a poetry workshop.

Everyone loves to receive flowers. These flowers and this beautiful card are from school children who have enjoyed taking part in Mrs Yorkshire's poetry workshops.

Mrs Yorkshire with her first grandchild,
Charles Michael Bailie, born 15th July
2020. Watch out for some Nannie-related
poetry in the future!

Coming Soon...
(Autumn 2020)

Mrs Yorkshire's Words of Wit & Wisdom

Following the huge success of her daily posts on social media, a book of hundreds of hilarious two-line poems for you to enjoy.

Coming Soon...
(Autumn 2020)

Mrs Yorkshire's Festive Words of Wit & Wisdom

A special festive edition of the Words of Wit & Wisdom. A two-line poem for every day from 1st December until 1st January and a bonus of four full-length Christmas poems.

Also available...

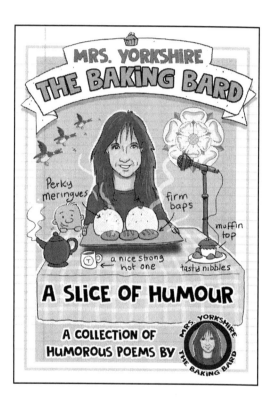

Also available...

Also available...

Mrs Yorkshire the Baking Bard
c/o PO Box 18
Ramsey
Isle of Man
British Isles
IM99 4PG

E-mail: carolellis2012@gmail.com
Facebook: Mrs Yorkshire the Baking Bard
Instagram: mrsyorkshirethebakingbard
Twitter: @mrs_baking
YouTube: Mrs Yorkshire the Baking Bard

Printed in Great Britain
by Amazon

35854511R00106